T0195866

# REACHING OUR YOUTH

Deante Jaheim Royster

Order this book online at www.trafford.com
or email orders@trafford.com

Most Trafford titles are also available at major online book retailers.

Print information available on the last page.

ISBN: 978-1-6987-1133-1 (sc)
ISBN: 978-1-6987-1131-7 (hc)
ISBN: 978-1-6987-1132-4 (e)

Library of Congress Control Number: 2022904072

*Trafford rev. 03/04/2022*

www.trafford.com
North America & international
toll-free: 844-688-6899 (USA & Canada)
fax: 812 355 4082

# Contents

This book is a guideline to help youth leaders, teachers, parents, and legal guardians reach the youth of today. This book will focus on topics that will enhance critical thinking from a biblical and mental standpoint. This book will also outline how you as a youth leader, teacher, parent, or legal guardian can help your youth be the best at being themselves as they can be. So let's get right to it, shall we?

# Chapter 1

# SETTING AN EXAMPLE

Have you ever sat back and heard the song "Practice What You Preach"? It's the same when you are around youth. The term "practice what you preach" simply means if you say something, then do it. It is important that you set an example to all youth, especially to younger children.

As you read, I want you to sit back and really think on this thought: Have I, as a youth leader, teacher, parent, or legal guardian, set a positive example for the youth around me? If your answer to this question is "yes," you also have to think about the following question as well.

Have the youth around me seen an example that could result in inappropriate behavior in the near future?

If the answer is "yes," it is more than likely the youth is meeting others, going to spend the night at a friend's house, or seeing something in a movie that could result in inappropriate behavior. The best thing to do is to make sure you show them the best example possible and monitor their behavior to see if the youth have picked up any other examples. When analyzing this, we must give the youth the freedom to make choices, whether the right choice has been made or not.

We, as a collective group of leaders, see that our youth are in a technologically-based world; anything the youth want to know or see can be found on the World Wide Web.

With the World Wide Web in the lives of our youths, they can easily see a bad example from others to emulate. For instance, if a celebrity is seen doing something that seems cool, then the youth want to follow or be like them.

As a minister, I tell the youth to be the best they can be spiritually, mentally, and physically. Being a leader and setting positive examples is very important. We must let them know that though they may want to be different, expressing similar behaviors of their peer group will not mean they are a "lookalike," but that they are still individuals.

So in this tech-based world, what can we do to help our youth see better examples?

First, we must be honest with them and let them know that they can share anything with us. If we do not imply this, then our youth will keep things bottled up inside, never letting it out, and be entangled on things they may be dealing with. As a result of this, the youth would turn to the world for answers, falling to temptations.

Second, we must stress it to the youth to watch the company they keep. We can see when the youth are around bad company. We sense it in many different ways.

One way we can sense improper behavior is how their company's attire looks. When someone does not grab a first impression with you far as the proper dress attire, then that's a red flag.

Another way to tell if someone is risky for the youth is how they talk, when someone uses a lot of profanity around the youth and do not have any regard for the youth in their presence. This will most likely lead up to the youth using the language. Why, you may ask. It's because the inexperienced mind of the youth would think it is acceptable. We have to attack these things at a young age. If not, we would be trying to address it in their teenage years, when they are most rebellious.

The youth do what appears to be cool in their eyes. Leaders have to show them the ropes of life, meaning show them that paying your bills and taking care of business is what is right and the best thing to do. You are going to get questions from the youth about these things, and you should give them your best positive advice.

The youth need us more and more each day.

Watching what youth wear as apparel is important also. They shouldn't be sagging their pants; young men, you are better than that. They shouldn't wear short shorts or dresses; young ladies, you are better than that. If you want to get far in life, it's further than sagging pants and short dresses and shorts.

What we as our collective group of leaders, allow them to wear and do not tell them otherwise, they will do it because they are getting attention.

One thing the youth do not recognize is when they get the wrong kind of attention.

It's up to us to be robust role models in their young lives. God has entrusted them to us as we are the positive people they

see day to day. So setting a positive example is very important in the lives of all youth. Let us collaborate with one another and think of various different ideas on how we can be positive examples to the youth.

# Chapter 2

# SHOWING LOVE

It is important to show love to all people, especially to the youth. I've found out that a lack of love shown to youth can result in many different reactions from them. The youth need us to show them love. So many youth are going through the problem of lack of love from family. A lot of modern-day homes have only one parent in them. When there is lack of love from family, say one parent is not in the lives of the youth, the youth turn to the world to fill that void in their lives. When a child doesn't have their mother, the empty void in their minds makes them seek that in a relationship. As we look at this common problem in most families and why a parent could be out of the picture in a child's life, there are many reasons why this is going on in modern homes.

When a child is brought into this world out of a relationship, both parents should come to a verbal agreement, if we separate from each other, our child needs both of us in their lives.

As we look at this picture, we have to think that this issue could also have a grand impact on the behavior of the youth.

The youth are frustrated when they don't have an answer from that parent that isn't in their life. One of the main questions I'm asked by many youth is, "Why doesn't my dad/ mom love me enough to at least call to check on me?"

And my answer to that question is, "If the parent wasn't shown love, when they have children it scares them and their mindset tells them to run away from there situation instead of facing their child saying, (I wasn't shown love, but I'm going to do my best to show you love the best I can."

All some children want is that love from family, and there is a lack of it from day to day in the modern homes. The lack of it in homes today isn't because the parent is not trying or the parents aren't trying, but it's because there is a lack of what they were taught. Love is the key in today's society. If the youth aren't getting the love from family, there needs to be a place that has mentors and counsellors to show love and fill that void.

As we look at this love and the impact it has on our youth today, we must realize that it is going to affect their adult lives later on. There needs to be women who will step up to them and teach them how to be young women and how to carry themselves accordingly. There needs to be men to be male role models and to teach young men how to be a man and to be manly. When the youth look to fill the void of love in their lives, they look at different ways to cope with this. Some turn to gangs, others turn to a life of drugs and alcoholism. Showing love starts as a child, from the time they came out of the womb. Some parents feel as if they aren't doing enough for their child/ children. I just want to say if you are trying, then you are doing your best. Love is action and has to be shown to young people day in and day out. It's easy for anyone to say they love these youth of today and the men and women of tomorrow. When the youth is hearing this from peers, it's possible that they are telling them because they are aware that it is what their peers want to hear.

We must be careful not to speak harshly or out of anger or out of how the they can make us feel but know that our words as their leaders have the power to help strengthen, build, uplift, and establish our youth.

We must speak from a love standpoint. When speaking from love, no matter what the youth may say about you, you

can overcome their words against you because you know that this is what you want to do in life.

You must have a backbone when speaking to the youth. Love has to be the main focus on getting their attention. When evaluating this, the following are some of the questions that can help you reach out to the youth you are trying to connect with:

1.  Do I have patience? Answering this question should be easy. When you deal with the youth at large, it takes a certain level of patience to address them in love.

2.  Do I enjoy working with the youth? So you are working with the youth, and anyone working with the youth should enjoy working with them. The youth would know if you like them.

3.  Am I transparent with the youth? Youth find ways to connect with people who are honest with their own struggles. Just be honest with the youth, and watch how they draw to you.

As discussed previously, love is vital in young lives, and we got to show it.

When the youth are dealing with their various life situations, we got to be there and show them the love that's

missing to make them act out of themselves. Love is action, so love isn't spoken, but it's shown.

How can you show love to the youth? It's more than buying materialistic things. Sometimes all the youth want is attention from their parent or legal guardian.

As I look at a lot of youth's lives that I came across, I sit and I wonder if love was shown and they didn't feel it or if love wasn't shown at all. These scenarios do take place, and we are not always aware. When we aren't aware, we risk the youth turning to the world and the streets for guidance, and that is the wrong type of guidance and the last place we need them to be.

The youth face so much, and as a young youth leader they express better to me mor than they would someone older.

When they express said feelings, it can be multiple things. I just try my best to be there for the youth in my life and who comes into my life. God has done great things, and if only the youth can grasp the concept of what's really going on, things would be different. Love is just the most important thing, and when there is a lack of it, we must pick up on it and show it the best way we know how.

We must communicate with the youth and stress it to them that although we are hard on them, we only want the best in life for them. If we do not get them by showing them love, the world will do just that, and they will be lost souls. So now we must examine our approach in dealing with the youth. We must approach these young lives with care and show it day in and day out. Love is that thing we all need in our lives, and love will get us through the hardest days of our lives. The youth need love more and more each day. As we look at what this world is coming to, we have to show it in more than one way and be robust leaders in their lives. I always like to say the youth that do not get shown love grow up having no direction in life. Looking at some adults today, they act the way they do because they were never taught how to love. The world is the way it is because the standard of love was dropped and other things came into play. We have entertained this lack of love so long. There is a lot that must be done to restore it the way it's supposed to be. First, we must realize that showing love is better than speaking it. When you love someone, that doesn't necessarily mean spending money all the time. Love is more than a price tag. A lot of times the best way to show someone, especially the youth, that you love and care is to spend quality time with them, doing some things they enjoy doing. We have gotten so spiritual to the point we cannot even go out to a movie and enjoy it anymore. Let us go back to the basics with our youth and show them love and teach them the true meaning of love. Remember that to reach our youth, we

must show them love and give them our attention more and watch the behavioral issues be resolved. L-O-V-E—listening, overcoming, visualizing, and expressing—all these things are part of love.

Let us reflect on what the Bible says about love . . .

1 Corinthians 13:4–8 ERV

[4]Love is patient and kind. Love is not jealous, it does not brag, and it is not proud.

[5]Love is not rude, it is not selfish, and it cannot be made angry easily. Love does not remember wrongs done against it.

[6]Love is never happy when others do wrong, but it is always happy with the truth.

[7]Love never gives up on people. It never stops trusting, never loses hope, and never quits.

[8]Love will never end. But all those gifts will come to an end—even the gift of prophecy, the gift of speaking in different kinds of languages, and the gift of knowledge.

When we look at this, we must follow this guideline to loving not only the youth, but also one another. Love is key in

today's homes, and it's needed more in the homes where there is a lot of chaos to bring behavioral issues to a standstill. So let us remember to love through anything we face and love more and more each day.

Chapter 3

# BEING TRANSPARENT

When it comes to the youth, nothing gets their attention like transparency. The youth look for people they can share their deepest, darkest problems with, and they look for you to open that door for them to share your experiences with them. If the youth feels as if this is something transparent with you, then they will share some things with you.

When youth share private things with persons of interest they look for nobody to share what they are told.

When what they have told you gets out, you risk the chance of them never sharing anything with you anymore. We must talk to them calmly in the way we would want to be talked to. A lot of times we talk to the youth with aggression, and as a result, the youth shut down from us.

We must show the youth our lives haven't always been a life of goodness and great living. The way to do this is by being absolutely transparent with them when we show them our lives, meaning not holding back any of our life's struggles from them. If we had an addiction, we need to share it with the youth we lead. If we had a sexual pull, then we need to share it with them, and maybe sharing these things will help the youth with what they are facing from day to day.

Being transparent is the best way to reach out to the youth. As you open up and share the naked truth, they will respect that more. As I've shared my story with different youth, they say things like "Wow, I did not know you went through that," or "I did not know you dealt with that."

We got to be that example, and how can we be that if we aren't open with our struggles? Now do not get me wrong, there are parents, teachers, youth leaders, and legal guardians who are upfront with things they have been through. If that's you, I thank you for that, but there are those who are scared to tell their children they were molested as a child. There

are those who do not know how to show love because they were never shown love, and as a result, they cannot face their children with issues they still have or still dealing with as an adult, but let's get through our issues together. Think about it: If we say that to the youth today, how much more will they trust us! This thing called transparency is important, and it starts with us.

As we think on how we are going to be transparent with our lives, we must make sure we do not leave anything out. When we leave out vital details, we set ourselves up for the youth to distance themselves from us. The youth can tell who really cares through the lens of transparency, and if you aren't honest about your struggles, then you do not need to be concerned about their issues. The youth keep so much inside, like anger or something they feel they can't just express to anyone they know, and as a result, there is a lot of anger and other suppressed feelings building in them, and that sometimes makes them turn or leads them to a life of crime. We must make ourselves available to these youth. As I always say, there always is a sign of action before a reaction. There is always something that pushed these youth to the point of reacting out of themselves. We should be so transparent with them that they could look through us like a window. The ball to get the youth back is in our corner, but if we do not take action, and take it now, they will be further lost in this world. The world has everything to offer to these youth, and they can

be successful if we are truthful and honest with them from the jump.

Being honest with them will lead them to being honest with us.

Transparency is the key to getting the youth open up with their problems. The thing is that the youth feel that nobody understands them at all. The truth is that the youth do not know how to or cannot express their inner thoughts and feelings because they are feeling trapped. When we come together, we can better understand the youth by collaborating ideas on how to be more transparent with them.

Let us think on how important transparency really is. As we become more transparent, we look for the youth to open up to us on a personal level that they wouldn't have done otherwise.

When you as a parent are upfront with your child/children, you open a vault of opportunity for them to becoming open with you. It is important that the youth can express themselves through transparency, and it is needed to interpret their mindsets. The youth do not share a lot because they feel they will be judged or talked about, and this makes them feel bad. We have to embrace these various mindsets and love them through whatever they are facing if they choose to share it

with us. It is crucial that we do not pressure the youth to being upfront with us or telling us things. What we must do instead is to let them know that we are here if there is anything they would like to share, and in doing this, they will share small things at first too see if they can trust us, and if they can, they will share more. We also have to stress it to them that we aren't going to judge them but be firm with them on how they're acting and behaving.

Being transparent is just one of the many steps to take to get the youth to open up to us on a personal level. Things that they share with their peer group should be things they can share with us with no judgment. Although they feel that their peer group is the right ones to go to, they do not see that behind their backs, their business is the top subject.

If peer groups really cared about what these youth are going through, they would try to get them help.

True friends always show their friendship when they see what a friend is going through. They put themselves on the back burner to help said friend. The key point here is being transparent with the youth will lead to an open door or many open doors. We just have to be honest and be there for the youth day to day.

We should have nothing to hide from them. We may not know it, but the youth pick up on when there is something wrong with us. As we lead and mentor these youth, we have to let them know we make mistakes too but that we allow our mistakes to make us better and not bitter. As positive role models, we must show them that we are the first part-takers of what we say to them. How can we expect them to be honest with us when we lie about our own struggles?

Yes I said it, we don't be truthful about the things we've done: but we want them to tell us if its anything they are facing.

We have to do better. It starts with us. Let us be transparent and upfront with these youth.

# Chapter 4

# MEETING THE YOUTH WHERE THEY ARE

It is crucial that we, the leaders, meet the youth on their level. We must know and understand that each youth is different in their own way. We must approach John differently than we would Sam. It is like having different opinions, whether one likes the LA Chargers or the New York Giants. These youth are the same way. Each of them has problems, and we must approach them in love and never compare them to one of their peers.

What I've noticed from the youth I talked to is that they feel as if they are being talked about instead of talked to. The very first thing they say is "We are people too, and we deserve respect too."

I tell these youth that if they show any level of disrespect, then they will not receive any respect they feel they should get. When addressing each youth on their own personal level, we must approach them with something that interests them. For instance, if Joe likes basketball and he is failing a class in school, we can use basketball to reach him on an educational level. Why, you may ask. That is because the young mind will quickly focus on something of interest to them than on something that seems boring to them. Educational materials can be fun if teachers allow it to be.

The minds of youth today need it to be fun; if it is not fun, they will tune it out. So our approach must be to make education fun for the youth to meeting these youth on a personal level. One thing I've observed while I was in the occupational course of study (OCS), they made every assignment fun in many different ways. I think all teachers should make educational material fun for students to keep them focused. Fun activities shouldn't just be in special ed classes. It should also be in every type of class, be it grade school, college, or university. When we make learning fun, more students will enjoy it. It's like what a teacher once

told me: You should get into a career that you enjoy doing. Shouldn't we make school interesting for the youth too? When I speak of making school fun, I'm speaking more than extra-curricular activities.

We have to meet youth where they are and show them the way from there. They need us, and we are all that some of them have. So let us not look down on them but find a way to help them get through whatever they may be dealing with.

When it comes to meeting youth on their own levels, it is imperative that we do not push them away with things that are not of interest to them. The youth are out there, and we can get them to come to us and get them where they need to be if we make the right approach, but it starts with getting to know each individual. When we get to know the youth, we look for that vault of opportunity that I'm always speaking of. No two people are the same, and knowing this, we cannot use the same techniques for each youth. It's our job to find each personal interest and use that to grab each youth. When meeting youth on their level, you have to be in tune to the things they like, such as sports, gaming, hanging out, and many other things.

Meeting youth on their level takes a certain level of patience. If and when you take on these responsibilities, you have to look at the task at hand. These are young lives, and they are in our care. So let us get to know each youth personally

and use what we learn about each one to better reach them. Remember that they may be in their youth, but they are still somebody, and although they are young today, they will hold the world in their hands tomorrow. We must meet them where they are and show them the way. So will you join me in reaching our youth of today and the men and women of tomorrow?

Printed in the United States
by Baker & Taylor Publisher Services